My First Cat

Veronica Ross

Thameside Press

Distributed in the United States by
Smart Apple Media
1980 Lookout Drive
North Mankato, MN 56003

Text copyright © Veronica Ross 2002

Printed in Taiwan

ISBN 1-930643-72-1

Library of Congress Control Number 2002 141319

Designer: Helen James
Picture researcher: Terry Forshaw
Consultants: Frazer Swift and Nikki Spevack

10 9 8 7 6 5 4 3 2

All photography Warren Photographic/Jane Burton with the exception of:

Front Cover (main) & 17 Corbis/Joseph Sohm, ChromoSohm Inc;
4, 7 (B), 8 Animal Photography/Sally Anne Thompson;
13 Bubbles/Denise Hager;
15 Bubbles/Frans Rombout;
19 (B) 21, 23 Animal Photography/Sally Anne Thompson.

Contents

Your pet cat

Cats are very friendly animals and fun to play with.

Cats and kittens make great pets, but they do need to be looked after carefully.

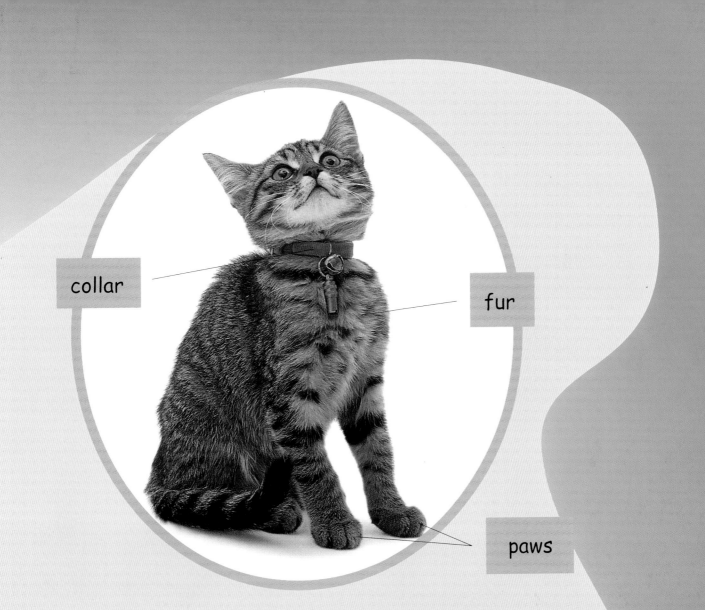

collar

fur

paws

A cat must be fed every day and its fur needs to be brushed regularly.

Young children with pets should always be supervised by an adult. Please see notes for parents on page 32.

What is a cat?

Cats belong to a group of animals called mammals. All mammals have warm blood, and fur or hair on their bodies. Cats like climbing and they can run very fast.

There are many different types of cat.

Tortoise-shell cat

Ginger cat

Some cats have long, fluffy hair.

Your pet cat is a member of the same family as lions and tigers.

Tabby cat

Choosing a cat

Grown-up cats can be just as friendly as kittens.

A kitten is very sweet and cuddly, but you will have to spend lots of time looking after it. An adult cat likes to do things on its own.

Animal shelters are good places to look for cats. You can buy kittens from breeders and pet stores.

Choose a cat that is friendly and lively, and looks healthy. It should have clean fur and bright eyes.

Kittens love to play and they will want you to play too.

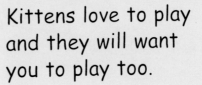

Settling in

Get everything ready
for your pet before you bring
it home. It will need a litter
box, food dish, and water bowl.

A blanket or cushion
inside a box or basket
makes a good bed.

Kittens like playing with a ball of wool.

Your cat will need some time to get used to its new home. Keep it in one or two rooms for the first few days.

Making friends

Most cats like to be stroked. They also like to have their head and ears rubbed.

Be gentle with your pet. Never pull its tail or tease it.

When you pick up your kitten, hold it around its bottom and chest.

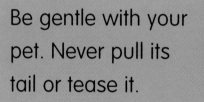

Your cat will
like sitting
on your lap.

If your cat is pleased to
see you, it will rub its
head against your legs.

13

Feeding your cat

You can buy special cat food
at pet stores and supermarkets.
The label on the can or box will
tell you how much to feed your cat.

Kittens need
four small meals
every day.

Make sure your cat always has a bowl of fresh water to drink.

A grown-up cat will eat two or three meals a day. Kittens can eat solid food when they are eight weeks old.

Cats are carnivores ("meat-eaters.") They need meat or fish to stay healthy.

Training a kitten

If you buy a kitten, you must teach it to use a litter box.

Put the box in a quiet, private place.

If your cat does something bad, say "No!" in a firm voice.

When your kitten has finished its meal, put it in its litter box. As soon as your kitten has been to the toilet, clear out the dirt.

If your cat has been good, reward it with a big hug.

Playtime

Cats and kittens enjoy playing. They like to crawl in and out of cardboard boxes, climb on furniture, and hide under tables.

If your cat scratches the furniture, buy a scratching post.

Put away any sharp things that may hurt your cat.

Make a house for
your pet out of a box.

Cats like to play
at hunting.

Keeping clean

You can help your cat
keep clean by brushing its
fur once a week. Use a special
brush and comb from a pet store.

Brush your cat
from its head
towards its tail.

Long-haired cats may need to be brushed every day.

Cats lick their fur to keep it smooth and clean, and use their paws to wash their face.

When cats wash themselves, they swallow loose hair. This can form a hair-ball in the cat's stomach and make it feel sick. If this happens, take it to the vet.

The outdoor cat

Cats love to go exploring outdoors. Make sure your cat always wears a collar with your telephone number on it.

Your pet's collar should be made from elastic.

Most cats like to climb trees and run along the branches.

Cats have a good sense of balance and hardly ever fall.

If you have a kitten, do not let it out until it has had all its injections.

Understanding cats

You can learn a lot about your pet by watching and listening. You will soon understand what it wants when it purrs or meows.

If your cat feels safe, it may lie on its back.

When your cat is happy, it will hold its tail in the air and purr. When it is frightened or angry, it will arch its back to make itself look bigger.

24

Stay away from your pet when it looks angry!

Your kitten will soon get to know the sound of your voice and your smell.

A healthy cat

You will need to take good care of your cat to make sure that it stays fit and healthy. If your pet doesn't want food, sneezes a lot, or has runny eyes, it may be sick. Take it to see the vet.

If your cat is scratching, it may have fleas.

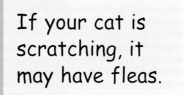

As your pet grows older,
it will sleep more.
Bigger cats still like being
stroked and talked to.

Make sure your pet doesn't eat
indoor flowers or plants as they
may be poisonous.

Visiting the vet

A kitten should be taken to see the vet when it is 12 weeks old. The vet will give it some injections to stop it catching any diseases. It will need extra injections every year.

The vet is giving this kitten an injection.

Kittens should be neutered when they are about five months old. This operation stops cats from having babies.

Take your cat to the vet in a special carrier, like the one shown.

Words to remember

animal shelter A home for unwanted pets.

breeder A person who sells animals.

fleas Tiny biting insects that live in a cat's fur.

hairball A ball of hair that forms in a cat's stomach.

injection A way to protect animals against illness.

litter box A cat's toilet.

mammal A kind of animal. Mammals have fur on their bodies and feed their babies milk.

meow The crying noise that a cat makes.

neutering An operation that stops cats having babies.

purr The noise that a cat makes in its throat.

vet An animal doctor.

Index

Notes for parents

If you decide to buy a cat for your child, it will be your responsibility to ensure that the animal is healthy, happy, and safe. You will need to make sure that your child handles the cat correctly and does not harm it. You will also have to train your cat and look after it if it is sick. Here are some points you should bear in mind before you buy a cat or a kitten:

• A cat costs money to feed. As it gets older, you may have to pay vet's bills as well.

• All cats should be neutered.

• Cats need injections every year. Can you afford them?

• Do you know someone who will look after your cat when you go on vacation?

• Is your home suitable for a cat? Do you have a backyard?

• Cats often bring other animals, such as birds and mice, into the house.

• Cats can be microchipped to identify their owners. Some people think this is safer and more reliable than wearing a collar.

• If you have any questions about looking after your pet, contact your vet.